PUDDLES AND PONDS

Books by Phyllis S. Busch and Arline Strong

Puddles and Ponds

LIVING THINGS IN WATERY PLACES

by Phyllis S. Busch

Photographs by Arline Strong

THE WORLD PUBLISHING COMPANY

CLEVELAND AND NEW YORK

All the photographs in this book are by Arline Strong with the exception of the following, which are reproduced here by courtesy of the National Audubon Society: on page 20, by Jeanne White; on page 23, by Leonard Lee Rue; on page 24, by Clifford E. Matteson; on page 26, by Allan D. Cruickshank; on page 27, by C. G. Maxwell; on page 29, by Robert Lamb; on page 32, by Alvin E. Staffan. The photograph on page 13 is reproduced by courtesy of the City of New York Department of Sanitation. The publishers gratefully acknowledge permission to use these photographs.

Published by The World Publishing Company
2231 West 110th Street, Cleveland, Ohio 44102
Published simultaneously in Canada by
Nelson, Foster & Scott Ltd.
Library of Congress Catalog card number: 75-82768
Text copyright © 1969 by Phyllis S. Busch
Illustrations copyright © 1969 by Arline Strong
Designed by Jack Jaget

TO JUDY FOR BENJAMIN

AUTHOR'S FOREWORD

This book is planned to encourage the very young child to experience his environment esthetically as well as intellectually—with his heart as well as his mind.

The approach is intended to stimulate children to learn by inquiry rather than by mere passive acceptance of stated facts. Thus the child is led to explore and to discover for himself the wonders and beauty of the world of nature.

Puddles and Ponds describes a pond community. It is part of a series whose purpose is to present the elements of ecology, and it is designed by its method and content to contribute to growth in the field of environmental education.

Sunny days are dry days—fine outdoor play days.
Dark days often come, with rain.
Drops of water fall from the clouds, making everything wet—
plants, rooftops, streets, fields, animals, people.

Water makes puddles and water makes ponds.
The city has mostly puddles,
although you might find a pond in a park.

A puddle can form on the pavement
where there is a little depression or a hole,
or where a drainpipe empties its collection
of rainwater from a rooftop,
or under a dripping icicle turning to water
in the winter sunshine.

Puddles that form from melting snowbanks sometimes shine like mirrors.
Here you might see your reflection upside down.
Puddles do not last long on city streets.
Rainwater or melted snow water collects in the street gutters, which lead to sewers.
From there the collected water enters pipes.
The pipes empty the water into rivers, lakes, or oceans.

You can follow the water trail to a sewer
after a flushing truck has finished sprinkling water on a city street.
The puddles of water which remain are not deep.
They dry up quickly.

If you place a teaspoon of water in a saucer it will evaporate overnight
and you will not be able to see it any more.
Before a street puddle disappears it may be used as a drinking fountain
by a thirsty pigeon or sparrow or dog or cat.

If you stir up the bottom of a puddle, the water looks muddy.
Water picks up soil as it moves and drops it when it stops.
The heaviest particles fall at the outside edges of a puddle, and the
lighter ones toward the center.
Sometimes water carries enough soil to one spot for some plants to grow there.
Have you ever found plants growing near sewers on city streets?

In the country the land is unpaved and uneven—
the way the city used to be
before there were streets. There are
many more puddles in the country.

And there we also find larger pools of water, called ponds.

There are ponds in the meadow
with cattails surrounding the water.
There are ponds deep in the woods,
often shaded by willows.
Then there are farm ponds,
where cows may drink and people may fish.

There is a stillness about a pond.
You can feel how restful it is
when you sit quietly
at the edge of the water,
watching and waiting.

Take a deep breath.
Besides all the sounds of spring to hear,
there is so much to smell, to feel, and to see.
Listen.
What do you hear?
The scolding of a redwing blackbird?
The song of a spring peeper?
The splash of a fish?
The quack of a duck?
The rustling of the wind through the willows and cattails?

From spring to summer is a busy time at the pond.
There are many kinds of green plants in and around the water making food,
growing and increasing in numbers as the days get sunnier and warmer.
The pond looks greener every day.

Animals are feeding on these plants or on other animals,
and they, too, grow and multiply.
There are fish and frogs in the water,
insects on the water,
birds flying overhead,
water snakes hiding around the edges.

There is much activity all through the day, and even after the sun sets.
Explore the muddy borders of the pond for animal tracks.
They are your clues to night visitors and night happenings.
Here are paired marks made by a deer.
While you were asleep the deer came down for a drink, then wandered
farther out to munch the leaves and flowers of the yellow pond lily
and nibble on its roots, pulled up from the muddy bottom.
You might find signs of mink and foxes too.

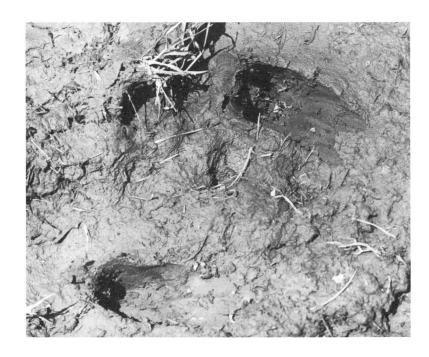

Little tracks which look like a baby's hand
were made by a raccoon.
It was probably looking for crayfish.

The crayfish is another night feeder.
In the daytime you might find one hiding under a stone
in shallow water at the edge of the pond.
All these creatures are seeking meals,
while each is careful not to become one.

Night life at the pond is filled
with sound as well as action.
The leaves, twigs, and branches swish,
flutter, and squeak in the night breeze.
You might hear the low melody of a
screech owl, the trilling of one toad or many,
or the spring song of a chorus of peepers
sounding rather like birds.

As you approach the peepers there is sudden silence.
If you wait quietly and patiently the music will start up again.
The trilling of frogs and toads is part of their courtship,
and courtship is followed by egg-laying.
Eggs are found near the shore and farther out,
in bunches or strings or singly on twigs and leaves.
They are blobs of light-colored jelly with dark centers.

After the eggs hatch, the pond teems
with tiny tadpoles busily feeding
on water plants.
Take some home with some pond water
and watch them grow.
At first the tadpoles look like little fishes
and many are eaten by turtles, fish,
and water insects.
The remaining tadpoles grow larger
and change into insect-eating frogs and toads.

Like a tall statue near the shore stands the great blue heron,
waiting to catch a tadpole, fish, or frog.

A snail crawls slowly at the pond's edge, searching for bits of food.
Suddenly it is gone—snatched by the heron.

In the open water paddles a duck—
a handsome male mallard.
He nibbles at the free-floating duckweed,
then suddenly turns bottoms up as he dives
for some nourishing pondweed.
Bright yellow warblers dart among the shrubs
searching for insects.
Frequently they pause to sing what sounds
like "Sweet, sweet. I am so sweet."

There are many other birds at the pond.
Here is a noisy kingfisher on a fishing trip.
You can see redwing blackbirds searching
for insects and spiders, or swallows
catching insects in flight.

Over the water fly the beautiful dragonflies,
insects with four colorful wings. Watch these acrobats darting about,
sometimes singly and sometimes
in pairs.

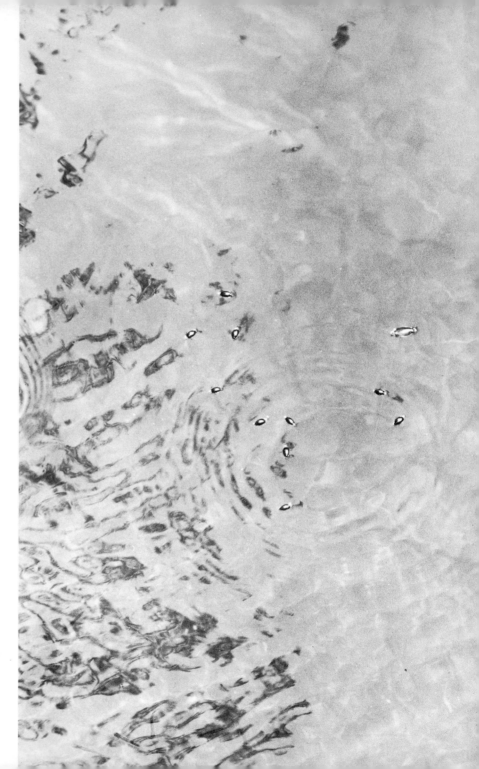

Not all the insects are in the air.
In the water you might find whirligig beetles
like these, going round and round,
or little half-inch back swimmers
paddling upside down.
Both eat smaller creatures.
You might see the thin water striders using
four of their six legs to ski
over the top of the water
as they hunt other insects for food.
They remain upright, bending the water film
but never breaking it.

Scoop some of the muddy water into a jar.
Add a piece of floating plant. Sniff it.
It has a pleasant smell.
After the mud has settled, start exploring.

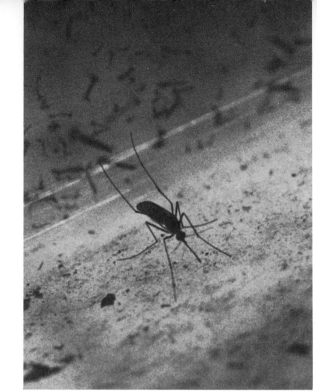

Look for water fleas—
tiny living dots which move quickly
up and down
on their invisible ten legs.
In the very early spring you might find the dainty inch-long fairy shrimp
swimming on its back, pinkish and almost transparent.
Female mosquitoes lay their eggs on the water.
When these hatch the active young larvae called "wrigglers" emerge.
Swimming among the wrigglers you might find dragonflies with their powerful jaws,
and immature caddis flies in their little tubes.
Mosquitoes, dragonflies, and caddis flies leave the pond when they become
adults, returning only to lay their eggs.

Large white water lilies float amidst their shiny dark green leaves, called lily pads. A lily pad often supports a resting frog.

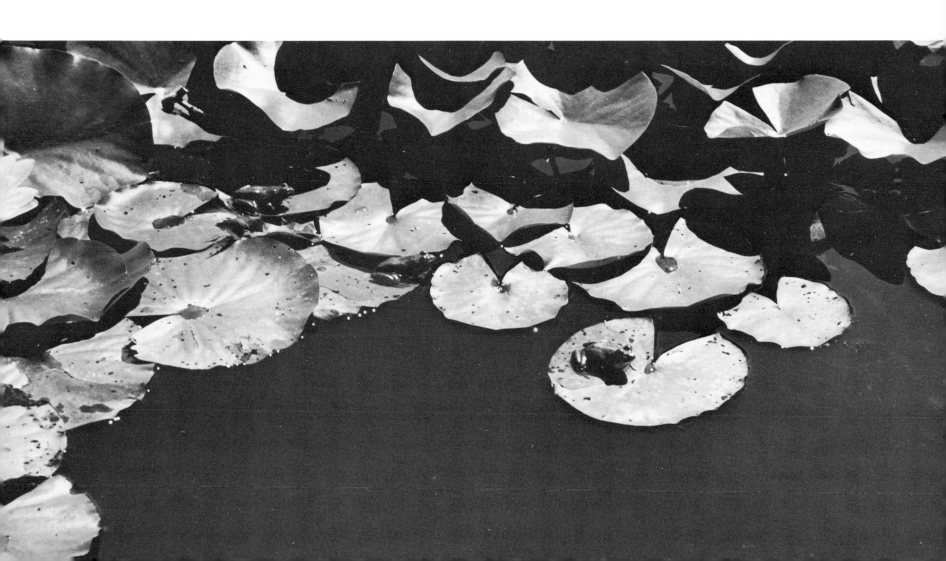

The water lilies open up in the early morning sunshine to make a fragrant flower show.
At this time they have many busy insect visitors.
Then early in the afternoon the water lilies close, to reopen the next sunny day.
Explore the underside of a lily pad. Place it in a shallow pan of pond water
so that you can search this new world of interesting things, such as snails, snail eggs,
beetle eggs, and a variety of fastened animals like dainty little flowers.

There is much to discover during the warm months,
but soon this time is over.
The days get shorter and cooler and
there is less sunshine.
Green plants make less and less food
until some stop altogether.
Frogs prepare to spend the winter
buried under the mud.

So do turtles.

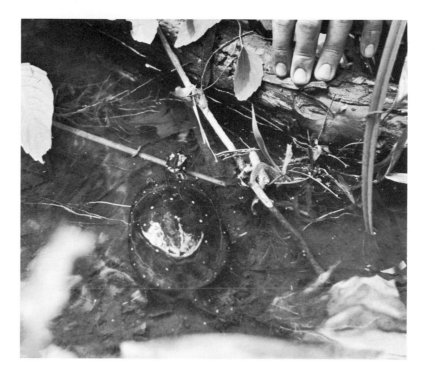

Beavers prepare for winter by building lodges—mounds of sticks and mud.
Their winter food supply of sticks is stored on the muddy pond bottom,
which they can reach through underwater exit holes from the lodge.

Most of the birds fly south,
but some linger awhile.
A Canada goose may stop at a pond
where it can swim, feed, and rest
even when the weather becomes very cold.

Then one night the pond freezes over, and suddenly the goose is gone.
Leaves on trees and shrubs around the edge of the pond change color,
making brilliant reflections in the water before they fade and fall.
As the weather gets colder and colder, ice begins to form,
first around the shallow edges, then all across the pond.

New ice is clear as glass.
You can look right through it
and see fish swimming below.
Sometimes the ice gets thick
enough for people to walk
and skate on it.

Now you can hear the sounds of winter—the crunchy,
whistling sounds of ice, snow, and bare branches.
You can smell the sweet fresh frost,
feel the chill breeze,
and blink at the snow crystals in the sun.

One March day you may spot the first flower
at the pond, poking through the snow.
It's the skunk cabbage,
with its hood colored green and dark purple-red.
Perhaps it even has a visitor inside,
an early bee making its first visit.

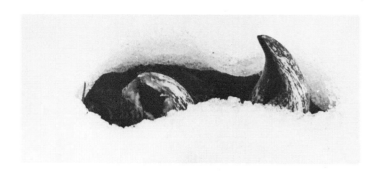

There is a stir of activity among all the living things in and around the pond.
Now you know that winter is not forever and that the pond will soon be
a livelier place.

ABOUT THE AUTHOR

PHYLLIS BUSCH, who is a science teacher, received her training at Hunter College, New York University, and Cornell University. The author of many publications on science and conservation, she has taught at every level—elementary school, junior high school, high school, college, and graduate school. Dr. Busch is Executive Director of New York State's federal project SPRUCE (Science Project Related to Upgrading Conservation Education). She and her husband live in Stanfordville, New York.

ABOUT THE PHOTOGRAPHER

ARLINE STRONG's photographs have illustrated many handsome science and nature books—among them another World book, *When the Tide Goes Out* by Helene J. Waddell. Her pictures have appeared in a number of exhibits and displays, including a one-woman show at New York's American Museum of Natural History. Originally a fashion photographer, she became interested in photographing nature as a result of her two sons' fascination with the world of science. She and her family live in Riverdale, New York.

I   2   3   4   5   73   72   71   70   69

8338